To my children

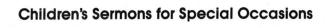

Children's Sermons for Special Occasions

CHILDREN'S SERMONS

FOR SPECIAL OCCASIONS

Roy E. De Brand

BROADMAN PRESS
Nashville, Tennessee

Unless marked otherwise, Scriptures are quoted from the Revised Standard Version of the Bible, copyrighted 1946, 1952, © 1971, 1973.

Scriptures marked KJV are from the King James Version of the Bible.

Scriptures marked NIV are from the HOLY BIBLE *New International Version*, copyright © 1978, New York Bible Society. Used by permission.

Scriptures marked Phillips are reprinted with permission of Macmillan Publishing Co., Inc. from J.B. Phillips: *The New Testament in Modern English*, Revised Edition. © J. B. Phillips 1958, 1960, 1972.

Dewey Decimal Classification: 252.53

Subject Headings: CHILDREN'S SERMONS / / HOLIDAYS—SERMONS

Library of Congress Catalog Card Number: 82-72228

Printed in the United States of America

Foreword

Roy E. De Brand loves children. His weekly sermon for these favorite friends attracts a crowd of little listeners eager to devour his every word. They are never disappointed.

That Dr. De Brand has something worthy to say is evident on every page of this little volume. His thoughts are timely, interesting, helpful, but above all biblical. More than mere object lessons, these are insightful sermons based upon God's Word.

Let the reader proceed with confidence! Blessings await all who meet these ideas first in print and then in various settings of worship, class, or even Vacation Bible School.

C. W. BESS, Pastor
Central Baptist Church
Jacksonville, Texas

Preface

Originally I was supposed to write a children's sermon book jointly with my best friend, C. W. Bess. I got busy finishing my doctorate, then moving to a new church field. He went ahead without me. So, in a sense, this book is a sequel to his. I owe much to his encouragement, friendship, and the ideas we've shared together through the years.

This book wouldn't be possible without the constant help, support, and encouragement of my wife, Carolyn. My children, Brian and De Ann, have been excited about it. They're two of the reasons I'm such a believer in the importance of children's sermons.

Faith Phillips is not only an efficient secretary and typist; she is a tenderhearted friend and devoted Christian. I deeply appreciate her skills and sweet spirit.

Thanks also to Emily McDonald who helped with some of. the typing.

All of these children's sermons were delivered at the First Baptist Church of Americus, Georgia. When I became pastor of this great church, many of the members had never heard a children's sermon. I decided I'd do one or two a month, as I could work them in. Well, they were so popular, my congregation insisted on one every Sunday! I'm deeply grateful for the encouragement, receptivity, and openness to new ideas of my people. Their eagerness and enjoyment of these children's sermons has called for discipline and creativity to get one a week ready. It's been well worth it. I'm deeply grateful for the loving support from this great church that helped make this book possible.

I hope this book will make you think, laugh, and see God more clearly. If it will start one more preacher on the road to doing children's sermons or fuel the fires of creativity in one already doing them, it will be worth the effort.

God bless you and your children.

Contents

III. OTHER SPECIAL OCCASIONS

Introduction

Children are an important part of the church. This is evident from Jesus' keen interest in children. He loved them, used them as examples of faith, gave them access when others would have turned them away.

The children's sermon is an extension of Jesus' love, an affirming way to give children a special place in the church. It speaks to their needs on their level. A children's sermon is a marvelous tool for conveying spiritual truth. And the truth is, children's sermons are not only for the children! Many adults in my congregation confess they get more out of the children's sermon than the one intended for them. Little do they know I often take that into consideration in my preparation.

The first children's sermon I ever heard was presented by J. P. Allen at Broadway Baptist Church in Fort Worth, Texas. I was spellbound! He was masterful at it, and I learned from him. Many a Sunday I was sorely tempted to join the children at the front of the church. Rather than do that, however, I kept my position and learned from where I sat. Later I became Dr. Allen's associate pastor. I owe much to that relationship.

Soon, however, I began to develop my own style for children's sermons. I believe any sermon must be biblically based. If it isn't biblical, it isn't a sermon. It may be a nice story or an object lesson or have a great moral. But it must be biblical to be an authentic sermon.

I also grew fond of using objects to reinforce truth, to make the sermon memorable. Sometimes I can find an object inexpensive enough to give one to each child as a "memory maker." This really works. They associate the truth with the object. I've heard them make these associations years later. What a joy it is when that happens!

Children's sermon ideas and objects are everywhere. Potentially, everything can become an object for conveying spiritual truth. This means we who are looking for ideas must be on constant alert. Sometimes I see something I think I might use and get it, having no idea what I might use it for. Eventually an idea and text will come along that fits the object. That's a happy day. Sometime an object will sit for months. Then one day, it all comes together.

We who do object-centered children's sermons become "scrounges." It gets into your blood. We ask airlines, realtors, insurance agents, car dealers, fast-food chains, in short anyone who has something to give away for "just enough for my kids." Then we live in mortal fear we'll be one short some Sunday. I've already planned what I'll do if that ever happens. I'll wipe away the child's tears and say, "I'll get you one!" And hope the child understands.

One of the best resources for children's sermon objects is a vending machine supplier. Unfortunately, they're rare outside of big cities. But when you find one, he'll have hundreds of inexpensive objects, packaged in quantity.

Don't persuade yourself that children's sermons are easy. They're hard work, but they also afford you an opportunity for creative expression of God's truth. They'll tax you, but they'll also bless you.

The children will especially love them. Children's sermons give this special segment of our congregation a sense of belonging in worship. What else in a traditional worship hour is for them? Not the hymns. Not the anthem. Not the sermon. Just this. Especially for them. It gives them pride and affirmation they need at this particular time in life.

I call the children to the front of the sanctuary about midway through the service. I seat them on the floor facing me, away from the congregation. This removes their desire to look around for Mom and Dad and wave. I demand their attention and respect. Sometimes that means I have to stop and say, "Listen!" Or remind them, "I do the talking; you do the listening." I frequently ask for their eyes and ears to be fastened on me. If you lose discipline, their attention goes with it.

Brevity is of the essence. The children's sermon should be three to five minutes—no longer. Be brief; be bright; be brisk; be right. This takes prayer, practice, preparation, and patience. But it's rewarded.

The children will love you for doing children's sermons. They may forget the texts and some of the main truths applied to the objects. But they'll not forget you. Children's sermons establish a rapport unattainable by any other medium. When they are ready to come talk to you about salvation or when they need to talk to you about a problem, you won't be the "stranger behind the pulpit." You'll be their children's sermon pastor. They'll come freely.

And when they're ready to profess Christ and join the church they'll be more at ease. They've walked that aisle many times. They'll be less nervous because of it.

The congregation will love you for doing children's sermons. In loving their children, you love them. Children's sermons will give the rest of the congregation added sensitivity to the children's presence and needs. So often the children are taken for granted.

Almost all children's sermon books are general in nature. This one deals specifically with ideas for special occasions. There are those uniquely Christian celebrations—Advent, Brotherhood Sunday, Christmas, Easter, Good Friday, the Lord's Supper (in alphabetical order). There's no denying the genuineness or deep meaning of these occasions. I hope these children's sermons will make them even more meaningful.

Then, there are those days recognized as special in our nation which we must claim for our Lord. I hope the section on national celebrations will help you interpret Father's Day, Halloween, Independence Day, Labor Day, Memorial Day, Mother's Day, New Year's, Thanksgiving, and Valentine's Day in a Christian context.

The third section is a catchall. We need to help our children deal with times of great sorrow. We need to teach them missions and stewardship. They need to learn of God's love and their responsibility in light of it. Seasons have special meaning and messages. So this final section of the book deals with special occasions of these types—fall season, grief, missions emphasis, self-image, spring season, and stewardship.

I
CHRISTIAN CELEBRATIONS

Advent

Brotherhood Sunday

Christmas

Easter

Good Friday

Lord's Supper

1
Advent
(Preparation for Christmas)

Good Things That Become Bad

Test: 1 Corinthians 10:23, "'All things are lawful,' but not all things are helpful. 'All things are lawful,' but not all things build up."

Main Truth: We must remember the main reason for Christmas is to celebrate Jesus' birth.

Interest Object: A bottle of baby aspirin.

* * *

As we get ready for a great celebration of Christmas I want us to think about the meaning of 1 Corinthians 10:23. Paul wrote, "'All things are lawful,' but not all things are helpful. 'All things are lawful,' but not all things build up."

Paul knew God created all things good. But sometimes even good things can be used in wrong ways and can become bad.

I learned this lesson one time when my son was sick. We gave him two baby aspirin to help him feel better. Well, he just figured on his own that if two would make him feel better, a whole bottle would make him feel great!

After we put the aspirin bottle on a high shelf in the kitchen and got busy doing something else, Brian climbed up the cabinet and ate all ninety-eight remaining aspirin!

Since it was a lethal dose, we had to rush him to the

hospital and have his stomach pumped out. He didn't like that one bit! He also learned not ever to take any medicine we didn't give him.

Now, aspirin isn't bad. It was invented to help us when we're sick, but too much aspirin is very bad and can even kill you! This is a case of something good becoming bad.

As we get ready for Christmas we must remember the main reason for Christmas is to celebrate Jesus' birth.

I like all the things associated with Christmas—Santa, the food, presents, special TV shows, songs, and carols. But if we forget the main reason for Christmas and just think about these things, they are good things that become bad.

The main reason for Christmas is to celebrate the birth of Jesus Christ. If you think of all those other things and forget Jesus' birthday, then those other things become bad. Remember, as you get ready, the real reason for Christmas is to celebrate Jesus' birth.

2
Brotherhood Sunday
(Interpersonal Relations)

Learning the Rules

Text: John 15:12, "This is my commandment, that you love one another as I have loved you."

Main Truth: If we follow Jesus we must love everyone as he did.

Interest Object: A poster with rules for school classroom behavior. (You can either borrow one from a teacher or make your own.)

* * *

On PTA night, my wife and I visited our daughter's classroom at school. On the wall was this big poster. These are the rules for classroom behavior.

Don't yell in the bathroom.

Only two at the pencil sharpener.

Whisper in the cafeteria.

Don't keep your hand up when the teacher is talking.

Be quiet in the library.

Use good manners.

There would be no learning without rules. If all the students in a classroom just did what they pleased, whenever they wished, the classroom would be bedlam. No learning could take place. So you have to learn the rules in school.

We need to learn rules. They're important in school. They're also important at home. We need to know what to do or not do to live together happily. They're important in our city and state and country. If there were no rules, people could drive as fast as they wished and our streets would be unsafe. They could take things from others without laws or rules saying not to.

We even have rules for children's sermon. I talk. You listen. All eyes and ears must be on me at all times. You don't come up here to play with friends or look back at Mom and Dad. You come to look and listen to me, or you don't come for children's sermon. Those are the rules.

We need rules in our faith too. Jesus had rules. He must have, because he said, "If you love me, you will keep my commandments" (John 14:15).

Well, we love Jesus. So we want to keep his commandments. A commandment is a rule, something we must do. We must follow the rules of Jesus.

What did he command? Well, the biggest and most important commandment he ever gave is John 15:12. He said, "This is my commandment, that you love one another as I have loved you."

Wait a minute! You mean that's all we have to do to follow Jesus? Love one another? That's simple!

But he said, "Love one another as I have loved you." That's not so simple, because Jesus' rule says we must love one another selflessly, like he did. He always put others ahead of himself. We have to love like that. He loved sacrificially. Jesus always gave of himself to others. He even died for others. We have to love people, all people, that much. And Jesus loved people with understanding. He always knew their needs and hurts. He also loved others forgivingly. No matter what they had done, he forgave.

So Jesus gave us the biggest and most important rule in the world. If we're to follow Jesus we must love everyone as he did. Everyone. No matter what their color, condition, or circumstances are. As he did. Selflessly, sacrificially, under-standingly, forgivingly.

Learn this rule of Jesus and put it into practice this week!

Three Kinds of Pearls

Text: 1 Samuel 16:7, "For the Lord sees not as man sees; man looks on the outward appearance, but the Lord looks on the heart."

Main Truth: You can't judge people by appearances.

Interest Object: A pearl.

Memory Maker: If you have an old string of artificial pearls lying around the house or can find one at a garage sale, unstring them and give each child one pearl.

* * *

You see that I have in my hand a pearl, but none of you knows how much this pearl is worth. It might be worth 5¢; it might be worth $500; and it might be worth $5,000. Unless you're an expert, you can't tell just by looking at this pearl how much it's worth.

That's because there are three kinds of pearls. There's a natural pearl, made by an oyster when a grain of sand or some other foreign matter gets into its shell and irritates a special membrane it has. The oyster forms layers and layers of pearl around this irritant. As those layers build up over months and years a natural pearl forms. They are very rare and expensive.

A second kind of pearl is called a cultured pearl. It's also made by an oyster, but it's made from an irritant a person puts into it. Cultured pearls are grown in large quantities, mainly in Japan. They're not cheap, but they are not as expensive as natural pearls.

Then, there's an artificial pearl, which this one happens to be. It's just a glass bead, painted to look like a pearl. It's not worth much.

You can't tell by just looking whether a pearl is natural, cultured, or artificial. You have to know what's on the inside.

This is also true with people. You can't judge people by appearances. You have to know what's inside them. You can't tell what people are like by whether they're pretty or ugly, fat or skinny, rich or poor looking, black-, white-, yellow-, brown-, or red-skinned. You have to get to know people before you can appreciate their true value.

Let's learn to look at people as God does, at the inside. 1 Samuel 16:7 says, "For the Lord sees not as man sees; man looks on the outward appearance, but the Lord looks on the heart."

To know the value of a person, like a pearl, you have to know what's on the inside. You can't tell by looking. You can't judge people by appearances!

3
Christmas

God with Us

Text: Matthew 1:23, " 'Behold a virgin shall conceive and bear a son, and his name shall be called Emmanuel' (which means, God with us)."

Main Truth: Through Jesus we see God's love clearly.

Interest Object: Plain card with the words "I Love You" printed too small to be read from more than a few inches away. One magnifying glass.

Memory Maker: A magnifying glass for each child. Inexpensive ones are available from vending suppliers or even retail.

* * *

I have a message for you this morning. I want you to be sure and get it, so I wrote it on this card. Here it is (hold up card). What? You can't read the message? Well, it's important, and I sure do want you to get it.

Here's a magnifying glass. It makes small things look bigger. Let me hold it up to this important message. Can you read it now? That's right! It says, "I love you!"

That's the message I wanted you to get. I love you. I wrote it small, but you can read it when it's magnified.

God's message to us is, and always has been, "I love you." But how could he best get this message to people?

Well, the answer is found in the meaning of Christmas. Jesus came to earth as a person to give all people God's message, "I love you!"

When Jesus was born, God became flesh and dwelt among us. God poured himself and all his love into the person of Jesus. God sent Jesus to magnify his message, "I love you."

Through Jesus we see God's love clearly. Everything Jesus did and said from the cradle to the cross, from birth to resurrection, shows us God's love. That's what Jesus came to do. That's the meaning of Christmas.

Before Jesus was born an angel came to Joseph in a dream and told him, " 'Behold, a virgin shall conceive and bear a son, and his name shall be called Emmanuel' (which means, God with us)."

Jesus was God with us. He magnified God's love. Through him we see God's love clearly. And that's why we celebrate Christmas!

I have a magnifying glass for each of you to help you remember that through Jesus we see God's love clearly.

A Happy New You

Text: Luke 2:10-14, "And the angel said to them, 'Be not afraid; for behold, I bring you good news of a great joy which will come to all the people; for to you is born this day in the city of David a Savior, who is Christ the Lord. And this will be a sign for you: you will find a babe wrapped in swaddling cloths and lying in a manger.' And suddenly there was with the angel a multitude of the heavenly host praising God and saying,
'Glory to God in the highest,
  and on earth peace among men with whom he is pleased!' "

Main Truth: Jesus' birth means we can become new in him.

Interest Object: A book of Christmas carols or a hymnal opened to Christmas carols.

Memory Maker: Often booklets of Christmas carols are available through insurance agencies, funeral homes, or some other local businesses. Give a copy to each child.

* * *

We do a lot of singing at our house. Everybody sings. While we work or shower or even walk around, we sing.

We especially sing during special seasons like Christmas. Seems like a Christmas song is always on your mind during this special time of year.

I like to sing "Santa Claus Is Coming to Town," "Rudolph the Red-Nosed Reindeer," and "Jingle Bells." I also like to sing all the sacred Christmas carols like "Joy to the World," and "Hark, the Herald Angels Sing."

One song I like real well goes, "We wish you a Merry Christmas, we wish you a Merry Christmas, we wish you a Merry Christmas, and a happy New Year!" (Sing it if you can.)

Well, one day my daughter was walking around the house happy and singing that song. Only she didn't have the words quite right. What she sang was, "I wish you a Merry Christmas, I wish you a Merry Christmas, I wish you a Merry Christmas, and a happy new *you!*"

A happy new you. The more I thought about it, the more I realized that's what Christmas really means: a happy new you. Jesus' birth means we can become new in him. He came to bring us new love, new joy, new peace, and new hope.

Like the message of the angel in Luke 2:10-14 says, "I bring you good news of a great joy which will come to all the people; for to you is born this day in the city of David a Savior, who is Christ the Lord. . . . Glory to God in the

Highest,/and on earth peace among men."
I wish you a Merry Christmas, and a happy new *you!*

The Way God Gives

Text: John 3:16, "For God so loved the world, that he gave his only begotten Son, that whosoever believeth in him should not perish, but have everlasting life" (KJV).

Main Truth: God's gift of love is for everyone.

Interest Object: A small gift-wrapped box.

* * *

I have this beautifully wrapped box I would like to give to one of you this morning. Would anyone like to have it? (*All hands go up, of course!*)

You all would! But wait a minute. I have some conditions about who gets it. First, I want to give it to a girl. (All boys' hands go down immediately, disappointed.)

The girl I give it to should be at least nine years old (younger girls' hands go down).

I want to give it to a blond-haired girl who is at least nine.

This blond girl, over nine, should have blue eyes. Anyone here still meet all these conditions? (A few hands will still be up.)

Now this blond-haired, blue-eyed, at-least-nine-years-old girl should be named Sherri. Anybody here fit that? (Only one hand remains.)

One more condition. She must be my daughter! (Gives box to her.)

Now, did you notice how all of you were excited when I told you I had a gift to give? And each time I added another condition, some of you lost hope? When I said I'd give it to a girl, all the boys were disappointed. When I said "At least nine," all you younger ones were left out, and so on with each added category. Finally when I said she must be my daughter, everyone was omitted except one. And she got the box.

I can do this because I love Sherri De Ann in a special way. I love each of you too, but I love her differently because she's my only daughter.

Sometimes we give gifts like that, to special people with special conditions on our gifts.

But God's gift of love is for everyone! That's what Christmas is all about. Christmas reminds us that God sent Jesus, his only Son, as his gift of love, for everyone. No conditions.

We are reminded of this truth in John 3:16, "For God so loved the world, that he gave his only begotten Son, that whosoever believeth in him should not perish, but have everlasting life" (KJV).

By the way, the box is empty. But God's love is full and free for everyone. By believing in him, you can receive his gift of love for yourself!

4
Easter

Bumblebees Can't Fly

Text: Luke 18:27, "What is impossible with men is possible with God."

Main Truth: God did the seeming impossible when Jesus came back to life.

Interest Object: A bumblebee. This could be a real, live one, a picture of one, or a plastic or imitation one.

Memory Maker: Some book stores carry a plastic "Busy Bee" you could give to each child to reinforce the main truth.

* * *

A group of students in an engineering class were given a problem to work. They were given all the dimensions of a bumblebee and had to figure out whether or not it could fly. Only they weren't told it was a bumblebee.

All they knew was a body size and weight and the size and weight of the wings of this object. They built a model. They tested it in a wind tunnel. It couldn't fly.

When they were told that the dimensions belonged to a bumblebee, they said, "Well, according to all our tests, the bumblebee can't fly!" Its wings were too small for the size, weight, and shape of its body.

The only thing is, nobody ever told the bumblebee it can't

fly! So, it goes on gathering honey, pollinating flowers, and doing all the important things a bumblebee does. Flying anyway.

Now think about that in relation to Easter. A man died. He was fully dead. He'd been beaten, nailed to a cross, and stabbed. He really died there.

He'd been taken down and put in a tomb. A huge stone covered the door. Armed soldiers guarded it day and night. No way for a dead man to come back to life and get out of the tomb. Right?

Wrong! Jesus rose again. Because he was God, he had the power. God did the seemingly impossible when Jesus came back to life. But "What is impossible with man is possible with God." So said Jesus in Luke 18:27.

That's the meaning and message of Easter. God did the seemingly impossible when Jesus came back to life. And you'd better believe it!

Dying to Live

Text: John 12:24, "Unless a grain of wheat falls into the earth and dies, it remains alone; but if it dies, it bears much fruit."

Main Truth: We have Easter to celebrate the resurrection of Jesus Christ.

Interest Object: An Easter lily in full bloom.

* * *

Do you know what symbols are? A symbol is something that stands for something else. For instance, this is my wedding ring. It means I'm married. It's a symbol of the fact I'm married.

I want to talk to you about an Easter symbol. It's this Easter lily. It grows from a bulb that kind of looks like an onion. You plant it in the ground. In the springtime the bulb sends up a stalk, then leaves, then a bud, then a flower.

If you took this beautiful lily home and planted it, it would soon die. The bulb would stay in the ground, but the plant would die. Then, when next winter's chill is gone and the spring sun warms the ground, another stalk would grow from this bulb and the process would be repeated.

The flower looks like a trumpet. It announces spring, the renewal of life. It's used to symbolize Easter because Jesus, who died and was sealed in a tomb, rose again. The Easter lily looks like it's trumpeting, "Jesus is alive!"

Jesus once said, "Unless a grain of wheat falls into the earth and dies, it remains alone; but if it dies, it bears much fruit" (John 12:24). He wasn't talking about seeds. He was talking about himself. He was using a symbol.

I want you to know the true meaning of Easter. It's not flowers. It's not decorations. It's not baskets or Easter bunnies. It's not colored eggs. It's not pretty clothes. The meaning of Easter is that a man, Jesus Christ, died and came back to life three days later.

We have Easter to celebrate the resurrection of Jesus Christ. As you celebrate Easter with all these symbols, remember: they only stand for something else. And what they stand for is that Jesus Christ our Lord is alive forever, and he can live in you!

A Reminder of Easter

Text: Romans 10:9, "If you confess with your lips that Jesus is Lord and believe in your heart that God raised him from the dead, you will be saved."

Main Truth: Easter reminds us we're saved by our faith in the Living Lord.

Interest Object: A sand dollar. You can pick these up at a beach or buy them in shell stores in any beach resort area.

* * *

One of the wonderful things about our world is that God placed in it so many wonderful things to remind us of him. One of these is the sand dollar.

You get these at the beach. You sometimes find them on the sand or you dig for them near the shoreline. They're a kind of shell. Once an animal lived in them. They have several things that remind us of our Living Lord.

Look in the middle of the top side, and you'll see a tiny, five-pointed star. This might remind us of Jesus' birth. God put a special star in the sky to guide the Wise Men to see Jesus. The star shined on Jesus as a baby to help men find the light of the world, the light of God coming into the world.

Around the star are markings that look like the petals of a poinsettia, the flower of Christmas. This also reminds us of how Jesus came and how he blossomed as a boy and young man. He did wonderful things in the lives of people he met that helped them bloom like flowers.

Some sand dollars have five holes in them, like these. This might remind us that after Jesus lived on earth for thirty-three years, he was crucified. They nailed him to a cross. The holes remind us of the holes in his hands, feet, and side.

Turn the sand dollar over, and you have reminders of the rest of Jesus' story. For here you see markings that look like an Easter lily. It is a flower that blooms only in the spring. The petals are open, like the open grave three days after Jesus died and was buried. He rose again. That's the meaning of Easter and why we celebrate it.

In the center of the underside of the sand dollar is an open hole. This also might remind us of the resurrection. Jesus walked out of the tomb; the stone rolled away. The grave was open.

One of the most interesting things about the sand dollar is that if you crack it in two and break it open, inside are five tiny pieces of shell that look like doves. (Break it open and carefully dump out the doves.)

The dove is the symbol of the Holy Spirit. It's also the symbol of peace. That's why Jesus came, lived, died, and rose again: to bring us peace.

So the sand dollar reminds us of Easter, and Easter reminds us we're saved by our faith in the Living Lord. As Romans 10:9 says, "If you confess with your lips that Jesus is Lord and believe in your heart that God raised him from the dead, you will be saved."

I hope the true meaning of Easter comes to you. Only by believing in Jesus can you know the true peace of salvation.

5
Good Friday

Finish What You Start

Text: John 19:30, "When Jesus had received the vinegar, he said, 'It is finished'; and he bowed his head and gave up his spirit."

Main Truth: We must fully commit ourselves to Jesus who died for us.

Interest Object: Model or picture of space shuttle craft "Columbia."

* * *

I hope you saw the blast-off of the space shuttle "Columbia" on April 12, 1981. I will never forget it. Remember how spectacular it was?

I remember something about it I hadn't noticed in other space shots. About two minutes into the flight, the flight director told astronauts John Young and Bob Crippen, "Negative seats." That meant they couldn't use their ejection seats from then on. They were too high.

Then, four minutes into the flight, ground control told them, "Negative return." That meant Young and Crippen were going into outer space. Up until then they could have turned back to earth. Now they couldn't. They had reached the "point of no return."

What if John Young and Bob Crippen had started crying

and kicking and screaming, "I don't want to go"? It was too late. They had to go now.

It takes tremendous dedication and commitment to be an astronaut. They are great examples to us.

We need examples because we easily start things but often find finishing difficult. Even little projects like building models, playing sports, or helping Mommy and Daddy mean sticking to the finish. Big things ahead of you—school, marriage, jobs, even Christianity—demand dedication to the end.

Decide now you are going to be a person who finishes what you start. Don't be a quitter. Don't give up when the going gets tough. Stick to what you start to the finish. It's the only way to make life what it needs to be.

The greatest example of finishing what you start is Jesus. He went all the way for God and us, even to the cross. Some of his last words on the day he died were, "It is finished." (John 19:30). That means he did exactly what God sent him to do.

He did that for us. Let's go all the way for him! We must fully commit ourselves to Jesus Christ who died for us.

6
Lord's Supper
(or Baptism)

Out of the Ordinary

Text: Matthew 26:26-29, "Now as they were eating, Jesus took bread, and blessed, and broke it, and gave it to the disciples and said, 'Take, eat; this is my body.' And he took a cup, and when he had given thanks he gave it to them, saying, 'Drink of it, all of you; for this is my blood of the covenant, which is poured out for many for the forgiveness of sins. I tell you I shall not drink again of this fruit of the vine until that day when I drink it new with you in my Father's kingdom.'"

Main Truth: Sometimes what you see isn't the most important thing but what becomes of it.

Interest Object: A rather large piece of wood, like a two-by-four about two or three feet long. Any large stick or piece of wood will do, however.

* * *

If I asked you "What do I have in my hand?" you'd probably answer, "A stick or a piece of wood." And you'd be right.

What if I told you, though, that this is a baseball bat or a chair leg or one thousand toothpicks? You might scratch your head and wonder if I'm crazy.

But in the hands of a skilled woodworker, with time and loving care, this piece of wood could become just about anything!

The same thing is true with us. People look at you or you look at yourself and see just a little boy or a little girl. But when I look at you, I see tomorrow's doctors, lawyers, teachers, mothers, fathers, and presidents. You can become anything you want to be and are willing to work hard enough to become.

I thought about that in relation to this piece of wood and ourselves this week in preparing for the Lord's Supper.

In the first Lord's Supper, told about in Matthew 26:26-29, Jesus took ordinary bread and wine and made it symbolize, or stand for something wonderful. The bread stood for his body. The fruit of the vine stood for his blood. Together they remind us that Jesus died on the cross for our sins, our salvation. His body and blood, symbolized in the bread and juice of the Lord's Supper, mean our sins are forgiven through Jesus.

Sometimes what you see is not the most important thing, but what becomes of it. Think about that this morning as we remember Jesus in the Lord's Supper.

Note: You could also use this idea with baptism, changing the analogy from bread and wine to ordinary water.

Something to Remember By

Text: Luke 22:19, "Do this in remembrance of me."

Main Truth: The Lord's Supper reminds us of what Jesus did for us.

Interest Object: A wedding ring.

* * *

This is my wedding ring. It's a reminder to me of a special occasion, a special person, and a special meaning.

The occasion? On December 22, 1963, I stood in front of a bunch of friends and family members and married Carolyn June Hayes. It was the beginning of our life together. That's special! This ring reminds me of that.

The person? My wife. Well, *now* she is. At first she was just another person, though I liked her a lot. We grew to love one another. Then we decided to get married and spend the rest of our lives together. So this ring isn't just a cold piece of gold. It's a reminder of this special person.

The meaning? It means love and faith and commitment to one another. It means that even on days when we don't feel close to each other or maybe we're mad or hurt, we're still married. And that's a special relationship. That's one thing that will never change. For our lifetime this ring is something to remember by.

Now here before us on this table are some pieces of bread and little cups, but they aren't just bread and cups. They're reminders of a special occasion, a special person, and a special meaning.

The occasion? The first Lord's Supper. Jesus and his followers were in an upper room having supper. He took some ordinary bread and an ordinary cup and gave it to his men and said, "Do this in remembrance of me" (Luke 22:19).

The person? Jesus Christ. He was their leader and their Lord. He wanted them to remember him always, even after he died. So he gave them the bread to remind them of his body given for them. And he gave them the cup to remind them of his blood, shed for them.

The meaning? The Lord's Supper reminds us of what Jesus did for us. He gave his life for our salvation. He died and rose again to give us eternal life. Each time we take the Lord's Supper we remember Jesus. It's what he gave us to remember him by.

When you take the Lord's Supper today, if you are a baptized believer, you remember Jesus. That's why he gave it to us. "Do this in remembrance of me."

II
NATIONAL CELEBRATIONS

7
Father's Day

A Father's Guidance

Text: Ephesians 6:1-2, "Children, obey your parents in the Lord, for this is right. 'Honor your father and your mother.'"

Main Truth: We should honor our fathers because God gave them to guide us through life.

Interest Object: A compass.

Memory Maker: A small, inexpensive compass for each child. These are available through vending suppliers or retail stores.

* * *

One way not to get lost in the world is to have a compass. You see on this compass that it has north, south, east, and west. It also has a magnetized needle that always points north. You line up the needle with the N and you can tell which direction you need to go. Then you won't get lost in the world.

There are other ways to keep from getting lost in the world. We have two fathers to guide us through life.

One is our Heavenly Father. God. He guides us through life. When we feel sad, alone, helpless, God is there. God's job is guiding us through life. He helps us so we don't get lost in sorrow, don't get lost in our problems, don't get lost in sin and stay lost. God helps and guides us through life. Like a compass always points to north, God always guides us in the right direction.

Most of us also have an earthly father to guide us. God gave us daddies to help us in life. When you have a problem, when you're hurting, or have a need, your dads will help you. They will guide you. Like God, they love you, care for you, and want only the best for you. God gave them to us to see that we are pointed in the right direction and guided through life.

This is Father's Day. We should honor our fathers because God gave them to guide us through life. Be thankful for your Heavenly Father and your earthly father. Tell them you're thankful for them. Tell them you love them.

Ephesians 6:1-2 says, "Children, obey your parents in the Lord, for this is right. 'Honor your father and your mother.'"

On this Father's Day, let's honor these God has given us to guide us through life.

8
Halloween

What Does the Devil Look Like?

Text: 2 Corinthians 11:14, "For even Satan disguises himself as an angel of light."

Main Truth: The devil disguises himself to make you do wrong.

Interest Object: A Halloween mask of the devil, plus any other devillike objects such as a pitchfork. I found a small plastic one at a department store. Or you could just use a picture of the devil. Or you could really get creative and get someone to dress up like a devil.

* * *

Do you dress up on Halloween and go trick or treating? Many people do. They dress up like ghosts or goblins, pirates or princesses, clowns or cowboys. Some even dress up like the devil. You know who the devil is: Satan. The Bible calls him the ruler of darkness, the tempter, the evil and wicked one. He's God's enemy, and he's ours.

But what do you suppose the devil looks like? Do you think he has a long red suit, horns on his head, a long, pointed tail, and carries a pitchfork? That's the way he's always pictured, and we think of him like that.

But the devil doesn't wear a red suit or have horns or a

47

pointed tail or carry a pitchfork. What does the devil look like?

Well, the devil can look like a lot of things. He can look like something you'd like to have but don't have the money for, and so you steal it. Or, he can look like something you shouldn't use, like liquor or drugs or dirty books. Or he can even look like another person, maybe even a friend, who tempts you to do wrong. The devil, our enemy and God's, can disguise himself to look like anything that can cause you to do wrong. The worst part about the devil is he always makes bad things look good.

That's what 2 Corinthians 11:14 means when it says, "For even Satan disguises himself as an angel of light." Don't look for the devil in a red suit with a pitchfork. Look for him when something you know is wrong looks good, and you're tempted to do it anyway.

The devil disguises himself to make you do wrong. Don't fall into his trap. Keep your eyes on Jesus Christ and follow him. Then the devil, whatever he may make himself look like, will be defeated!

9
Independence Day

The Badge of Discipleship

Text: John 13:35, "By this all men will know that you are my disciples, if you have love for one another."

Main Truth: Love shows people we follow Jesus.

Interest Object: An American flag lapel pin.

Memory Maker: American flag lapel pin or decal for each child. You can get these at banks, insurance companies, or civic organizations as promotional items. They're usually more than willing to let you have enough when you tell what they're for.

* * *

I believe all Americans ought to be proud of our country. We need to love America and show our love for our country. But how do we show our love?

One way is to wear the flag on your lapel or collar or jacket. I proudly wear the colors this morning, and I want you to wear them too.

Don't ever be ashamed to say, "I love America." It isn't a perfect land, and the people aren't perfect. But America is a great nation, and you can be proud and love it.

You show your love for our country not only by wearing her flag, but also by obeying her laws, serving when called on, always speaking highly of our land, and loving your fellow Americans.

The same thing is true in Christianity. Just as your love shows your patriotism, love shows people we follow Jesus.

In John 13:35, Jesus said, "By this all men will know that you are my disciples, if you have love for one another."

We don't all wear lapel pins to show people we follow Jesus. Our love is our badge of discipleship. We show our love by obeying Christ, serving in his church when called on, always speaking highly of our Lord, and loving all people. Don't ever be ashamed to say or show "I love Jesus." Your love is your badge of discipleship.

It's a Grand Old Flag

Text: Psalm 33:12, "Blessed is the nation whose God is the Lord; and the people whom he hath chosen for his own inheritance" (KJV).

Main Truth: We must give thanks to God for our freedom.

Interest Object: Flag of the USA.

Memory Maker: A paper bookmarker with this text and a picture of a flag, Bible, and cross is available at many book stores. They are inexpensive, and the children love them!

* * *

On this Fourth of July weekend I want to talk about our country and our grand old flag.

Our flag stands for something. It is a symbol of freedom. We've had a US flag since 1777, the year after we won independence from England. George Washington, the father of our country, once told what the flag stood for in his mind. He said the blue reminded him of the heavens and that our country is founded on faith and is responsible to God. The red reminded him of the flag of England and that our roots and heritage were in Great Britain. The white reminded him of liberty. Since the white stripes came between the red, they reminded George Washington that though we came from England, we were separated and now free.

The colors also mean something to me. The red reminds me of blood. Red is the color of blood. I think about how many Americans gave their lives so we can be free. I hope you're never called on to die for your country. But we are called on each day, as red-blooded Americans, to keep our nation strong by working hard, loving our country, and being good citizens.

The white reminds me that others not only fought, but taught and thought about how to keep America free. White is the color of a page in a book. That reminds me that education is a key that unlocks oppression and ignorance. Learn to like to read so you can know the truth that makes you free.

The blue and the stars remind me of God. We are free today because God gives us freedom. We must keep our faith in God strong, keep church and state separate, keep religious freedom strong.

When you look at our flag you may think of different things than these, but always remember this. Our grand old flag is the symbol of a free nation. We must give thanks to God for our freedom.

As a reminder to you to thank God for our country, I want you to have this bookmark with Psalm 33:12 on it, "Blessed is the nation whose God is the Lord" (KJV).

10
Labor Day

The Greatest Tool Ever Invented

Text: Ecclesiastes 9:10, "Whatever your hand finds to do, do it with your might."

Main Truth: God gave us hands to work for him.

Interest Object: A tool box or tray with assorted tools.

* * *

What is the greatest tool ever invented? Maybe it's the hammer (hold up one). With the hammer we can drive nails, pull them out, and knock things loose. It's a great tool.

Perhaps, though, the pliers are the greatest tool. You can twist and turn things with pliers and push and pull.

Or maybe the screwdriver or the adjustable wrench or the tape measure is the greatest of all tools (hold each tool up as you mention it).

Personally I think the greatest tool ever invented is far older than any of these. In fact, the greatest tool is not made by human hands at all. It *is* the human hand, the hand made by God.

God gave us hands to work for him. Our hands contain fifty-four of about two-hundred bones in our bodies. This tool, the hand, makes all other tools work. The hands are the greatest tools because they were invented by God and given to us to work for him.

Ecclesiastes 9:10 says, "Whatever your hand finds to do, do it with your might." This means our hands are to be busy hands, and helpful hands, and praying hands.

God gave us hands, the greatest of all tools we have to work with. Let's use them for him.

11
Memorial Day

Something More Important Than Life

Text: John 15:13, "Greater love has no man than this, that a man lay down his life for his friends."

Main Truth: We must remember that there are some things more important than life, and honor those who died for them.

Interest Object: An American flag.

Memory Maker: An American flag or flag lapel pin or sticker for each child. These are readily available from banks, businesses, and patriotic organizations.

* * *

Do you think anything is more important than being alive? Well, the plain truth of the Bible and of our nation's history says that there is.

This is Memorial Day weekend. Tomorrow is a holiday in honor of all who served, and especially all who died, in our country's service. The fact that some have died for our nation means there are some things more important than life. Freedom, for instance. Many gave their lives in two World Wars, Korea, and Viet Nam that we might be free.

Truth is another thing more important than life. Many people have died in the struggle of truth over falsehood.

Peace is another thing more important than life. It seems strange to say that some have to die in war in order for there to be peace, but it's true. We live in peace today because soldiers fought and died to win it.

Jesus knew there were things more important than life. In fact, he gave his life that we might have salvation, forgiveness of sins, and peace with God. And he came back to life to prove that he had the power of life and death. We have life through him. Let's live our lives for Jesus each day.

Jesus once said, "Greater love has no man than this, that a man lay down his life for his friends" (John 15:13). He did that for us, and others have given their lives that we may live in freedom, truth, and peace.

We must remember that there are some things more important than life and honor those who died for them. Take a few moments tomorrow to think about that. And then display this American flag I'm going to give you with pride and in honor of those who died that we might live.

12
Mother's Day

Hearts and Treasures

Text: Matthew 6:21, "For where your treasure is, there will your heart be also."

Main Truth: No thing is ever as important as a person.

Interest Object: Junk toys like those vended in machines. You can buy these cheaply from a vending machine supplier.

Memory Maker: One junk toy for each child.

* * *

One time I saw something in a restaurant that reminded me of something Jesus said. On this Mother's Day, it would be good for us all to think about it.

At the door of the restaurant there was a vending machine. You've seen them. Sometimes they hold bubble gum or peanuts or candy. This one sold junk toys, like these (hold a couple up).

As this family was leaving the restaurant, the little boy went over and began to look at the machine and twist the knob. He went over to his dad and asked for a quarter. Dad said no. So did Mom.

The little boy went back and twisted the handles some more. When his parents reached the door to leave they called for him. He wouldn't go. "I want a quarter," he demanded.

"No," was the answer.

Then he begged. Still no. Then he cried. Then screamed.

His mother went over and grabbed his hand. He resisted. She pulled. He kicked her. She slapped him. He yelled, "I don't love you anymore!"

I thought, *Boy, sometime soon I have to tell my boys and girls at children's sermon about what's important and what isn't.*

No thing is ever as important as a person. I thought about that in the restaurant, watching that family. And I thought about what Jesus said in Matthew 6:21, "For where your treasure is, there will your heart be also."

The little boy's treasure was the junk toy. At that time, it was more important to him than his own mother. Because of that, he hurt his mother's feelings and got hurt himself.

His treasure should have been in his mother more than the two-cent toy they sell for a quarter. If he'd been minding, listening, and loving then neither of them would have been hurt.

Boys and girls, the most important things in the world are God, family, and friends: always people, never things.

Remember that on this Mother's Day, and each day, and both your hearts and your treasures will always be in the right place.

I'm going to give you one of these toys to help you remember—no thing is ever as important as a person.

Sweetness Lightens

Text: Ephesians 4:32, "Be kind to one another," and Galatians 6:2, "Bear one another's burdens, and so fulfill the law of Christ."

Main Truth: Sweetness lightens life's burdens.

Interest Objects: One raw egg, an average-sized glass filled with water, a bowl of sugar, and a teaspoon.

* * *

I want to show you something very interesting this morning as we think about our mothers—how they treat us and how we should treat them.

On this tray I have a glass of water, a raw egg, and a bowl of sugar. Now watch what happens when I put the egg into the water. It sinks.

Now I'll take the egg out of the water with my spoon.

Next, I'm going to add a heaping spoonful of this sugar to the water. This is just ordinary sugar like you put on your cereal each morning.

Now an amazing thing has happened which can teach us a great spiritual truth. Look what happens when I put the egg into the sugared water. It floats! The sugar changed the water, and the egg now floats which sank in plain water.

You've all had days when things didn't go right at kindergarten or school or play. You go home feeling lousy. And what happens? Mother greets you with a smile and a kiss and makes you feel so good you forget what a rotten day it's been.

Mothers have learned that a little sweetness lightens life's burdens.

I think that's a lesson we need to learn and practice on our mothers. This day why don't you think of some sweet, loving act or words to lighten your mother's day? Tell her you love her. Clear the table for her after lunch, so she can sit down and read the paper. Take out the garbage without having to be asked or begged or threatened.

You'll find that a little sweetness on your part will lighten your mother's day, and it will lighten you and make you feel good too.

You'll be practicing what the apostle Paul wrote in Ephesians 4:32, "Be kind to one another," and in Galatians 6:2, "Bear one another's burdens, and so fulfill the law of Christ."

A little sweetness lightens life's burdens. Try it on Mom this Mother's Day, and on everyone else you see this week!

13
New Year's

The Old and the New Year

Text: 2 Corinthians 5:17, "Therefore if any man be in Christ, he is a new creature: old things are passed away; behold, all things are become new" (KJV).

Main Truth: We can live each new day as new persons if we put God first.

Interest Objects: A calendar from the old year just past—well marked and worn—and a brand new, clean, and clear calendar for the year ahead.

Memory Maker: A new year calendar for each child. Several businesses (banks, insurance companies, car dealers) in your area will have these to give as promotional items.

* * *

Here is my calendar for the year just finishing. I got to looking at it the other day and learned some things about the old year. It was busy. It went by so fast. Seems like it just got started; now it's over.

Many things on my old year's calendar made me smile. Some made me sad. Many good things happened. Some weren't so good.

The important thing to remember about the old year is that it's gone. Not a single day or second can be relived. No mistakes can be corrected. No joy reexperienced.

Here is my new calendar. There are a few things on it already. But for the most part, it's clean. Every day is new. No day of the new year has ever been lived before, and each new day is a gift from God.

What we do with each day of the new year is up to us. God gives us the opportunities. How we use them depends on us. We can live each new day as a new person in God if we put him first. He will make us new.

Put God first, others ahead of yourself, and self last. Then 2 Corinthians 5:17 can be said of you, "Therefore if any man be in Christ, he is a new creature: old things are passed away; behold, all things are become new" (KJV).

The Power to Run Our Lives

Text: Isaiah 40:29, "He gives power to the faint,/and to him who has no might he increases strength."

Main Truth: Our spiritual power comes from God.

Interest Object: A small battery, the kind that powers digital watches. You can get one from a jeweler.

* * *

Something interesting happened to me the other night. I was working at my house. I looked at my watch. *Good. Only 8:30.* I had plenty of time to finish my project. I kept working.

In a little while I looked at my watch again. *Plenty of time. Only 8:30.* I worked on.

I began to get tired. I thought, *It must be getting late.* When I looked at my watch it still said 8:30! *Uh oh.* I put it to my ear. No hum. The battery was dead.

The next day I took it to a jewelry store and got a new battery, like this one. It runs great again.

Life is sometimes like that. We need power to run on. If we don't sleep or eat or exercise right, we run down physically.

What about spiritual power? How do we get the strength not to sin when tempted, to be brave in life when sadness comes, to face problems, love God, attend church, pray? Where does our spiritual power come from?

It comes from God! Isaiah 40:29 says, "He gives power to the faint,/and to him who has no might he increases strength."

Remember that when your spiritual power runs down. God has power and will give it to you. You must ask for it. Pray for it. God will give you the power to run your life.

Remember that each day of this new year. Our spiritual power comes from God!

The Right Tools

Text: 1 Corinthians 13:13, "In this life we have three lasting qualities—faith, hope and love. But the greatest of these is love" (Phillips).

Main Truth: The right tools for living well are faith, hope and love.

Interest Object: One tiny screwdriver (the smaller the better), one huge screwdriver (the larger the better), and one board with the largest screw you can find partially screwed into it. Get two children to help you.

* * *

I have a problem this morning. Maybe you can help me with it. I need to screw this giant screw into this two-by-four.

62

Did anybody bring a screwdriver with you this morning?

(Have the small screwdriver planted on one of the children. The child is awaiting the question and will volunteer the screwdriver.)

Oh, good. Let's see, put the screwdriver in the slot. Hey, it's too small. In fact, the screw is bigger than the screwdriver. There's no way it will turn. It's the wrong tool. Did anybody else bring a screwdriver? Maybe a bigger one? (The second volunteer holds up the large screwdriver.)

Ah, this one will do. See, the screw is turning. This is the right tool!

Boys and girls, as we look together at a brand new year ahead we have to realize we can't live well, can't have a happy new year if we try to live it with the wrong tools. As we put together each new day, we can't face life with the tools of doubt, fear, and worry. Like the tiny screwdriver with the big screw, they're the wrong tools.

The right tools for living well are faith, hope, and love. If we apply these to daily living, we can have a happy new year indeed.

In 1 Corinthians 13:13, Paul said, "In this life we have three lasting qualities—faith, hope and love. But the greatest of these is love" (Phillips).

Make faith, hope, and especially love your tools for daily living, and you will live well in the new year!

14
Thanksgiving

The Lord Is Your Shepherd

Text: Psalm 23:1, "The Lord is my shepherd, I shall not want."

Main Truth: God provides for us in every way.

Interest Object: Plastic pilot's wings. These are available from major airlines. I've found that if you tell them what you want them for, they're more than happy to supply enough for each child to have one.

Memory Maker: Pilot's wings for each child.

* * *

Recently, I took a trip on an airplane. I was very tired when I got on the plane. Since my flight was going to be over four hours long, I thought I'd get some rest.

Shortly after we took off, the flight attendant came by with some soft drinks. I took one, and it helped me relax. Then she came by with some food. I ate.

After dinner, I took out a book I had brought along. Reading is very relaxing.

After we'd been flying about two hours, a flight attendant walked past me to the front of the airplane. She unlocked the door to the cockpit. Inside I could see the pilot, copilot, and flight engineer. They were very busy. There were all kinds of knobs and gauges and instruments all around them. They were glad to see the flight attendant with their hot coffee.

Then it occurred to me that while I drank and ate and read and relaxed, all those airline people were working hard for my safety and comfort. All I had to do was sit back and enjoy the flight. They were worrying about the weather, the plane, and the meals. I was thankful for them.

This is Thanksgiving week. Have you ever stopped to think about all the people who look after your needs each day? There are many: Parents; policemen and firemen; teachers. You could think of a dozen more.

But the greatest thought of Thanksgiving is that God watches over us and provides for us in every way.

David wrote in Psalm 23:1, "The Lord is my shepherd, I shall not want." That means God loves us and cares for us as a shepherd does his sheep. There is no need in our lives God does not provide for.

Isn't that a wonderful truth? We can be very thankful for it. God provides for us in every way.

Let me give you a pair of pilot's wings I got from the airline. Let them remind you that God is our pilot in life. He provides for all our needs.

If we can remember this and be thankful for it, our Thanksgiving will be the best ever!

Towers of Gratitude

Text: Luke 19:10, "For the Son of man is come to seek and to save that which was lost" (KJV).

Main Truth: We should be most thankful for what Jesus does for us.

Interest Object: Some junk like a flattened tin can, broken mirror, scrap of tile, seashell, broken bottle.

* * *

(Hold up pieces of junk taken from box or tray.) What would you do with this? Throw it away? I would too!

But recently I learned about a man who would have taken junk like this and turned it into an art treasure.

His name was Simon Rodia. He came to America from Italy in 1921. He was so thankful to be in the United States, free and happy, that he wanted to do something to show his gratitude. So he began to build a tower, a tower of gratitude.

But Simon Rodia was poor. He lived in Watts, the poorest section of Los Angeles, California. So he built his tower of gratitude with junk. He'd walk the railroad tracks near his home and pick up anything he could find—steel rods, seashells, broken bottles, bits of tile, or mirrors. He'd fashion these together with cement. He worked only in his spare time, and he worked alone.

Simon worked on his towers for thirty-three years! He built fifteen of them, beautiful and glistening above the grayness of Watts—marvelous towers of gratitude that stand today as art treasures for all to see.

It occurred to me as I saw these towers of gratitude that what Simon Rodia did with junk, God does with people.

Without God we are lost. Helpless. God picks us up and makes something beautiful of us by putting us in his kingdom.

That's what Jesus meant when he said, "For the Son of man is come to seek and to save that which was lost" (Luke 19:10, KJV). Jesus saves us from our lostness.

Of all the things we have to be thankful for at this Thanksgiving season, we should be most thankful for Jesus and what he does for us. He saves us.

Let's build towers of gratitude each day with our lives. Let's be living towers of gratitude for what God has done for us!

Waking Up the Gods

Text: Psalm 121:3-4, "He who keeps you will not slumber./ Behold, he who keeps Israel/will neither slumber nor sleep."

Main Truth: We are thankful for a God awake to all our needs.

Interest Object: Any kind of bell. The actual ones referred to in this message are like jingle bells on a string. The string is about the size of your fist. The bells can be any size or shape.

* * *

When my wife and I went to Japan we saw a curious sight. We were in a Buddhist temple. A man came in and knelt before this great big Buddha. A Buddha is a statue, an idol which the Buddhists worship.

The worshiper had a little sack with him. As he knelt before the Buddha, he reached into his sack and took out some bells on strings. He rang them three or four times (ring your bell). Then he clapped his hands loudly three times (clap your hands). Then he rang his bells again (ring yours). Then he did the same thing a third time (you do, too). Next, he began bowing and talking.

Well, I'd never seen anything like that before! I wondered what he was doing. So I found a Buddhist priest who spoke a little English and asked him.

"He's praying," the priest told me.

"Why the bell ringing and the hand clapping?" I asked. And do you know what the priest told me?

"He's waking up the gods so they will hear his prayers!"

Now, boys and girls, we have a lot of things to be thankful for this week. You could name a hundred things you're thankful for. But the thing I'm most thankful for, more than anything else in the whole world, is that we have a God who never sleeps. We don't have to wake God up to hear our prayers. We are thankful for a God awake to our needs.

The Bible says, in Psalm 121:3-4, "He who keeps you will not slumber./Behold, he who keeps Israel/will neither slumber nor sleep."

God knows our needs and provides for them. He never sleeps! Anytime we need him, he's always there—watching, caring, loving.

How thankful we can be during this Thanksgiving season for a God who is awake to all our needs!

15
Valentine Day

God's Love and Ours

Text: 1 John 4:7-12, "Dear friends, let us love one another, for love comes from God. Everyone who loves has been born of God and knows God. Whoever does not love does not know God, because God is love. This is how God showed his love among us: He sent his one and only Son into the world that we might live through him. This is love: not that we loved God, but that he loved us and sent his Son as an atoning sacrifice for our sins. Dear friends, since God so loved us, we also ought to love one another. No one has ever seen God; but if we love each other, God lives in us and his love is made complete in us" (NIV).

Main Truth: We are Christians because of God's love and show it by our love.

Interest Object: Some Mexican jumping beans.

Memory Maker: Jumping beans for each child.

* * *

As we think of love this Valentine's season, I want to talk to you about God's love and ours. This is what 1 John 4:7-12 says, (read text; it's too long to quote).

These verses tell us God is love, God loves us, we ought to

love God, we ought to love one another, and we ought to love all people.

Let me illustrate this truth with a Mexican jumping bean. Some beans about this size grow in Mexico. Inside each bean lives the larva of a small moth. When it moves around, the bean actually moves and jumps.

These jumping beans I have today aren't real Mexican jumping beans. These are plastic with a ball bearing inside. But they give you the idea of a real jumping bean (let it roll around in your hand). These beans jump because something is inside them.

These verses I read tell us we're Christians because something is in us. It's God's love! And we show we're Christians by our love.

God loves us. We must love God. We must love others.

In this season of love, let's let love fill us and move us—God's love and ours!

Where Is Your Heart?

Text: Matthew 6:21 says, "For where your treasure is, there will your heart be also."

Main Truth: You learn to love the things you value.

Interest Object: A valentine-type heart.*

Memory Maker: Valentine-type hearts for each child.

* * *

We talk a lot about hearts around Valentine Day. Of course, we all know the heart is really just a muscle, about the size of your fist, in your chest that pumps blood to all parts of your body.

But we think of the heart as the place in us where our love and feelings are. We say to one we love, "I give you my heart," "My heart aches for you," or "I love you in my heart." We hear songs about cheating hearts and broken hearts. We send cards shaped like hearts.

Jesus talked a lot about the heart. He urged people to give their hearts to God or to let him come into their hearts. He told the Pharisees they had evil hearts. He told his disciples, "Let not your heart be troubled" (John 14:1).

But the most important thing Jesus ever said about the heart was in Matthew 6:21 when he said, "For where your treasure is, there will your heart be also." He meant you learn to love the things you value. Whatever you think is important in life you learn to love.

Where is your heart? What are the things you value and love and treasure?

Let me tell you some things you should value and love. God. Parents. Your home and family. Other people. Yourself. Learning. Reading. And the right kind of things, not sinful and harmful things.

Keep these values in your heart, and your heart will always be in the right place.

*(When I first did this one, I had some inexpensive key chains with a plastic valentine-type heart on them which I showed and gave as a memory maker. You can sometimes find them at a vending supply company in bulk at a reasonable cost. Or you could use valentines or even hearts of red construction paper.)

III
OTHER SPECIAL OCCASIONS

Fall Season

Grief

Missions Emphasis

Self-Image

Spring Season

Stewardship

16
Fall Season

"Whatchagunnado?"

Text: Mark 4:1-20. Read many times in your favorite version and summarize it for the children.

Main Truth: Our faith grows strong in Jesus Christ.

Interest Object: An acorn.

Memory Maker: An acorn for each child.

* * *

In Mark 4:1-20, Jesus told a story about a farmer planting seeds. Some of his seeds were eaten by birds. Some were burned up by the sun because they fell on shallow, rocky soil. Some were choked by weeds. And some grew into strong and healthy plants that gave good crops.

Jesus compared the seeds to the way people hear his word. Some people don't stick with Jesus and thrive and grow. Others plant themselves deeply in his word and grow and help others to grow.

I thought of this Bible story the other day as I heard a strange sound on my roof and patio. I'd hear something go, "Click, click, click, clop." Then, a few minutes later, I'd hear it again.

When I went to check it out, I found out the sound was

from acorns falling onto my roof and bouncing down to the patio: "Click, click, click, clop."

In the fall season the acorns fall off the oak trees. If they fall onto good ground and get plenty of rain and sunshine, they grow into oak trees. Mighty oak trees grow from tiny acorns.

Others just lie around on patios or rocks or in areas too wet or too shady until they crack and wither and die.

Hey, acorns are a lot like people! If we plant ourselves in Jesus Christ, absorb the light of his Word, drink in his teachings, send roots deep into his love, we grow strong in spirit and faith. If we don't we become withered, less than we ought to be.

Reminds me of a poem I read once:

> Hi there, acorn.
> Whatchadoin', acorn?
> Whatchagunnado, acorn?
> Grow into a mighty oak, acorn?
> Or crack and wither away, acorn?
> Hey, acorn,
> Is that my face I see in you?

Christopher Erickson
(From DECISION © 1969 by The Billy Graham Evangelistic Association)

17
Grief

God's Strength

Text: Psalm 46:1, "God is our refuge and strength,/a very present help in trouble."

Main Truth: God gives us strength when we need it.

Interest Object: One metal rod and several (eight to ten) sticks about the same length as the rod. I used an automobile jack handle for the rod and cut up a cane pole for the sticks. Any old rod and sticks will do, however.

* * *

I'm holding a stick. I could break it in two very easily. What if I add another stick? I can still break them with no trouble.

When I add several more sticks, I can still break them, but not as easily. Look at what happens when I add a whole bunch of sticks. They would be very difficult to break.

Now, what if I put a steel rod into the middle of all these sticks? There's no way I could break them, ever. Strength has been added beyond my own.

Let's say the single stick represents you or me. There are a lot of things that could happen in life to break us—to hurt us—and make us feel all broken up inside. Like when someone you love dies. Or when you have to move and leave all your friends. Or when you do something that hurts those you love and you feel rotten about it. Or when you fail in something you really wanted to do well in.

These are things that make us feel broken. It's easy to break when you're all alone. We need other people to give us strength. We need family and friends. That's like adding these sticks. It makes it harder to break. We need the support and fellowship of the church. This makes the sticks even stronger.

But still, they're pretty fragile. Is there anything or anyone who can make us so strong nothing can break us?

Yes! There's God. He can be a steel rod of strength within us when we call on him for help and trust him.

The psalmist wrote, "God is our refuge and strength,/a very present help in trouble" (Ps. 46:1).

That means God gives us strength when we need it. And we all need it. Let God be your strength, and troubles can never break you!

Lessons from a Popped Balloon

Text: Ecclesiastes 3:1-2, "For everything there is a season and a time for every matter under heaven:/a time to be born, and a time to die."

Main Truth: We must learn to deal with all of life's real experiences.

Interest Object: A popped balloon.

Memory Maker: A balloon for each child.

* * *

Not long ago I took my children to the Ringling Brothers and Barnum and Bailey Circus. It really was "the greatest show on earth."

I told the children they each could have one souvenir. Brian picked a gun that shot sparks. De Ann picked a huge, pink balloon with a clown's face on it.

She loved that balloon. She played with it for a couple of weeks. When it would lose air, we'd blow it back up, and she'd play with it some more.

One day as she was playing with it, it popped. I guess it was just worn out. Well, she cried and cried. She was heartbroken. So we sat down in my rocking chair and had a long talk.

I learned some lessons that day from a popped balloon. That was a real experience, and we must learn to deal with all of life's real experiences.

We talked first about a Scripture, Ecclesiastes 3:1-2. It says, "For everything there is a season, and a time for every matter under heaven:/a time to be born, and a time to die." Then we talked about three lessons we learned from the popped balloon.

First, we have to remember that no object lasts forever. There's a time for everything. Things last only for a little while, then they're gone. Nothing on earth lasts forever. Everything begins and ends—balloons, even human beings. We're born. We live. We die. Nothing lasts forever.

Second, we talked about how all of life's experiences aren't happy ones. When something or someone we love comes to an end, it makes us sad. When the balloon pops, a toy gets broken, or a pet gets run over, we're sad. This is especially true when a person, like grandmother or grandfather, dies. We must learn that all of life's experiences aren't happy.

You're going to have some sadness in life. It will come. And you should know it's okay to feel sad, to cry, to ache inside. If you didn't care, you'd never get sad. All of life's experiences aren't glad and happy.

A third lesson from the popped balloon is that the most important things in life aren't material possessions. What is important? People. And feelings. And, most importantly,

God. God is most important because he made all things and sees us through all life's experiences whether good or bad. He is in control of everything. And he loves us.

So we must trust our God of love whenever we're sad. By doing so, we can learn to deal with all of life's real experiences.

I want each of you to take one of these balloons to blow up after church. And when it pops, learn from it. No thing lasts forever. All of life's experiences aren't happy. And the most important things in life aren't things—they're people, feelings, and God. He will help you handle your heartaches!

18
Missions Emphasis

God Is Love—Not Wood or Stone

Text: 1 John 4:8, "God is love."

Main Truth: We must know and share the good news that God is love.

Interest Object: A Buddha or a picture of a Buddha.

* * *

This is a Buddha. A Buddha is an idol or a representation of a god. Millions of people all over the world bow down before Buddhas just like this one every day. They worship them. They pray to them. It's the only god much of the world knows anything about. They're made of wood or stone or metal.

When I was in Japan I saw lots of people worshiping Buddhas. In one place in particular I saw a woman really worshiping and praying. She looked like a woman with a problem. She was crying and had a very concerned look on her face. She'd kneel before her Buddha and pray, rocking up and down. Then she'd stand up and ring bells and clap her hands. She'd walk around to the offering box and toss coins in. Then she'd go back and pray to the Buddha some more.

My heart wanted my mouth to cry out to the woman, "Woman, that piece of stone doesn't hear your prayers. He's not a real god. God is love, not wood or stone!"

Oh, I wanted to tell her of the God I know. Our God is real, living, and caring. He's not carved out of anything. In fact, he's the Creator of everything.

Boys and girls, you must know our God is a God of love. We must know and share the good news that God is love. He told us to go into all the world and do that.

Some of you must go as missionaries to tell people in their own language that God is love. All of us can pray for those who go, and we can give our money to help send others. We can tell people we talk to that God is love. This is our job as Christians. Let's help tell the whole, wide world God is love—not wood or stone.

How to Get There

Text: Romans 10:14-15, "But how are men to call upon him in whom they have not believed? And how are they to believe in him of whom they have never heard? And how are they to hear without a preacher? And how can men preach unless they are sent. As it is written, 'How beautiful are the feet of those who preach good news!' "

Main Truth: Missions is telling people how to get to God.

Interest Object: Airline baggage tag.

Memory Maker: Baggage tags from airline.

* * *

Recently I took a trip on an airline. When I got to the airport, I checked my baggage in at the desk. I had one suitcase, two hanging bags, and a briefcase. There were two hundred or three hundred people on the same plane, some of them making connections to other flights going everywhere. Many bags looked alike. How could they tell where in the world mine were supposed to go?

Simple! When I checked my baggage at the desk, they put a baggage tag on it like this one. It tells the flight numbers, the transfers my luggage needed to make, and the final destination. And then, so I can tell my bags from everyone else's, it even has a number all my own for my luggage. This little tag tells all the airport people how my bags will get where they're supposed to be.

Missions does the same thing as this tag. Missions is telling people how to get to God. Some people do missions by being preachers, missionaries, and witnesses as they go. Others help send those who go by supporting them with their prayers and money. Both are important.

In Romans 10:14-15, Paul wrote, "How then shall they call on him in whom they have not believed? and how shall they believe in him of whom they have not heard? and how shall they hear without a preacher? And how shall they preach, except they be sent?" (KJV).

By our prayers and money and direct witnessing we can tell people how to get to God!

19
Self-Image

God Knows Your Name

Text: Matthew 10:30, "But even the hairs on your head are all numbered."

Main Truth: God knows everything about you.

Interest Object: Name tags. These can be anything from paper to leather luggage tags or anything in between.

Memory Maker: A name tag for each child. Inexpensive plastic ones are available from vending machine suppliers, or make your own!

* * *

Once I heard about a little boy saying the Lord's Prayer. Only he got it wrong. He didn't say, as you're supposed to, "Our Father who art in heaven,/Hallowed be thy name" (Matt. 6:9). Instead, he prayed, "Our Father, who art in heaven, how'd you know my name?"

That's funny! But it also reminds us that God does know your name. God knows the name of every person on earth, all four billion of us!

But there's something even more surprising than that. God knows everything about you. Matthew 10:30 says, "But even the hairs on your head are numbered." Can you imagine that? God knows how many hairs each of us has. Some of us keep him busy each day subtracting!

A God who knows your name and the number of hairs must know everything about you: all the good and bad; all that makes you sad and glad; all your hopes and fears, loves and hates. God knows. There's nothing about you God doesn't know.

A God who knows you that well must care a great deal about you. God loves you. That's why he knows about you. He loves you not because of your goodness but in spite of your badness. God loves you, just as you are. Warts and all!

And do you know what God wants? He wants you to know and love him. Know all you can about him. Love him as he loves you.

Take a name tag. It will help you remember—God knows your name and everything about you. He loves you. He wants you to know and love him.

How to Be the Kind of Person You Want to Be

Text: Luke 2:52, "And Jesus increased in wisdom and in stature, and in favor with God and man."

Main Truth: God will help you be the kind of person you want to be.

Interest Object: A growth chart, the kind you put on the wall to measure height by marking and dating. I got mine from a local realtor, but you can make your own if you can't find a preprinted one.

Memory Maker: A growth chart for each child, or at least an explanation of how they can make their own.

* * *

This is a growth chart. You hang it on your wall. Then, once every few weeks, you stand very tall against it and measure. Mark where the top of your head comes to. Then date that mark. The next time you check it, you can see if you've grown any.

Growing is a natural process. We grow. That's the way God intended it. It's helped by getting plenty of rest, eating the right kinds of food, and getting lots of exercise. So, we're all going to grow, naturally.

But how do you grow up to be the kind of person you want to be? Well, the Bible gives us some clues. Luke 2:52 says of Jesus, "And Jesus increased in wisdom and in stature, and in favor with God and man."

That means that Jesus didn't just grow bigger. He grew wiser and grew spiritually and socially. He grew to be the kind of person he wanted to be, and God wanted him to be.

How do we do that?

For one thing, get an early start. Jesus began as a boy. You don't live ten, fifteen, twenty, or twenty-five years and then suddenly, magically, be whatever you want. Life is a process of becoming. Start now when you're six, eight, ten, twelve to be the kind of person you want to be later.

Another thing: Don't get discouraged. Keep on trying. Don't give up easily. You must work hard to develop habits and traits you admire. Work on humor, patience, kindness, love. They don't come easily or suddenly. Get rid of things in yourself that you don't like in others. Never stop trying to make yourself better.

And ask God for help. He cares about you. He wants you to become the very best person you can be. When you fail, he forgives you and gets you started again. Trust God to be there to help you out.

God will help you be the kind of person you want to be. Try to be like Jesus. Then you'll never go wrong!

When We Rob Ourselves

Text: Matthew 16:26, "For what is a man profited, if he shall gain the whole world, and lose his own soul?" (KJV).

Main Truth: We rob ourselves when we put anything ahead of spiritual values.

Interest Object: A toy gun that looks very much like a real gun.

* * *

The newspaper carried a funny but sad story the other day about a man who went into a large bank to rob it. He handed the teller a note and a bag. The note instructed the teller to put all her money into the bag.

"I have a gun," the man said as he pulled one out. The only problem was, it was a toy gun. Though it looked very much like a real gun, the teller recognized it as a toy gun and called a guard.

The man was arrested and convicted for bank robbery and sentenced to twenty years in prison!

Now, I want to ask you something. Who did the man really rob? He didn't rob the bank. He got caught! Who did he rob?

He robbed himself! He robbed himself of twenty years of freedom. He robbed himself of whatever name and influence for good he may have had. Look at all he gave up just to try to steal a little money!

Boys and girls, we sometimes rob ourselves. You may think not, but we do. We rob ourselves when we put anything ahead of being like Jesus.

We rob ourselves when we think only of ourselves and not of others.

We rob ourselves when we do wrong instead of right.

We rob ourselves when we seek less for ourselves than what God wants for us.

We rob ourselves when we love things more than people.

Anytime we put anything ahead of God, of loving and serving him, it's like the man with a toy gun. We rob ourselves.

Jesus talked about this when he asked, "For what is a man profited, if he shall gain the whole world, and lose his own soul?" (Matt. 16:26, KJV). And the answer to his question is: NOTHING!

You only rob yourself if you lose your soul over anything. Don't rob yourself. Invest yourself by putting your faith in God and your interest in spiritual values. Anything else is self-robbing!

20
Spring Season

The Legend of the Dogwood

Text: John 3:16, "For God so loved the world, that he gave his only begotten Son, that whosoever believeth in him should not perish, but have everlasting life" (KJV).

Main Truth: Jesus died on the cross for our sins.

Interest Object: A branch of blooming dogwood, or an artificial one or even a picture of one.

* * *

This is dogwood, and there's a marvelous legend or story about it. Dogwood only blooms in the spring. It's supposed to be a reminder that Jesus died on the cross for our sins.

The legend of the dogwood says it once was a large, strong tree. Dogwood grew in Judea, near Jerusalem. The story goes that the cross upon which Jesus died was actually made of dogwood.

Because the dogwood was used for Jesus' cross and brought such sorrow, the legend says God cursed the dogwood tree. From then on it wouldn't grow large. It would forever be a scrawny, little tree. It is today.

The dogwood blossoms are supposed to remind us of Jesus' death. Look at this blossom. Two of its petals are larger than the other two. Kind of reminds you of a cross, doesn't it? Each petal has a dot on it. They're red, like blood. The center inside each blossom looks like a crown of thorns, like they put on Jesus. He died in the spring, the same time the dogwood blossoms.

Boys and girls, in springtime nature comes back to life. The trees burst forth with green. Dogwoods blossom. Grass greens and grows. Life seems to begin again.

Let the spring season and the legend of the dogwood remind us that Jesus died on the cross for our sins. But let us also never forget that he came back to life after death. As the dogwood lives on, so does Jesus. And we can live on with him, forever, through faith in him. Accept his gift of love on the cross for the forgiveness of your sins. Then you will know real life through Jesus.

This is what John 3:16 means. It says, "For God so loved the world, that he gave his only begotten Son, that whosoever believeth in him should not perish, but have everlasting life" (KJV).

21
Stewardship

Together We Can

Text: Acts 2:44, "And all who believed were together and had all things in common."

Main Truth: Together we can do what we can't do alone.

Interest Object: A barbell too heavy for one child alone to lift but easily lifted by three children.

* * *

I need some help. I need this barbell moved from here to there. Brian, come up here and move it for me. (He tries, but can't.)

Laura, you come try. (She tries, but can't.) Well, you almost did it.

Charles, would you come try? (Same unsuccessful story.)

Now, all three of you come back up here, please. Brian, you and Charles get on the ends. Laura, get in the middle. Now, each of you put both hands on the barbell and when I count to three, lift it together.

One, two, three, lift! (This time they're able to get it up.) All together you can lift it!

Together we can do things we can't do alone. Even if one of you could have lifted the barbell by yourself, it would have been too much of a burden to ask you to carry. Besides, if you lifted weights regularly and you were the only one who did, nobody else's muscles would develop.

Today we're going to vote on our church budget for the new year. It will be $250,000. Maybe one person could give it all. I can't. Even if I could, it wouldn't be fair to me or the rest of the congregation. Everybody needs to develop giving attitudes.

We need to exercise spiritually as well as physically. One way is by giving. One person or a few shouldn't do what we all should do together.

It takes all of us giving as God expects to receive the blessing and do the job he wants for us. Each does a small part. Each of us does what he can. All our money goes together, all parts of the church are supported, we all develop spiritually together, and our gifts reach out to all the world.

Together we can do these things we can't do alone. It's like the earliest Christians did. Acts 2:44 tells us, "And all who believed were together and had all things in common."

Together they did what they couldn't do separately. Many people were saved, and God's work prospered.

That's the way it must be in our church. Each of us must do our fair share of the work, witnessing, giving. Together we can do what we can't do alone!

What Is Treasure and What Isn't?

Text: Matthew 6:19-21, "Do not lay up for yourselves treasures on earth, where moth and rust consume and where thieves break in and steal, but lay up for yourselves treasures in heaven, where neither moth nor rust consumes and where thieves do not break in and steal. For where your treasure is, there will your heart be also."

Main Truth: Real treasures are spiritual, not things.

Interest Object: A piece or two of iron pyrite, fool's gold. You can get these from any rock collector or mineral shop.

* * *

Many years ago two young friends decided they'd spend their lives looking for gold. They sold the few things they had and went out West to look for gold. They looked and looked and looked, but they weren't too successful.

They found a little bit of gold. For over forty years they filled up a small bag. In the meantime, life passed them by.

One day, they were in a river panning for gold. One of the prospectors saw something shining in his pan. He took it out and washed it off. It looked like gold. He bit it to see if it was soft like gold. It was. He started to yell to his friend, "We've struck it rich!" Instead, for some strange reason, he put the nugget into his pocket.

Before the day was over he found three or four nuggets. He knew this was what he'd been looking for.

In the early morning, before his friend woke up, he got up and headed for town. He went straight to the land office and gave the whole little bag of gold he and his friend had collected for over forty years to buy the land with the river of gold.

As he turned to leave, his friend arrived. "You dirty rat, you found gold and kept it all to yourself. You're no longer my friend," he yelled.

The man who had bought the land went to the assayer's office to have his nuggets weighed and measured. He had found gold, bought the land, and was ready to become a millionaire.

The assayer weighed the nuggets, then tested them with chemicals. "I'm sorry," he said as he handed the man his nuggets back. "This is fool's gold, iron pyrite, worthless. Only an expert can tell the difference!"

What the man thought was treasure was worth nothing.

And it had cost him everything, even his friend of forty years.

What is treasure and what isn't? Jesus said in Matthew 6:19-21, "Do not lay up for yourselves treasures on earth, where moth and rust consume and where thieves break in and steal, but lay up for yourselves treasures in heaven, where neither moth nor rust consumes and where thieves do not break in and steal. For where your treasure is, there will your heart be also."

We think things are treasures—gold, money, houses, land, cars, nice clothes. But real treasures are spiritual, not things. You can't handle, buy, or sell real treasures.

Real treasures are spiritual gifts like friendship, love, hope, faith, God, church, the Bible. Seek real treasures: people, not things; giving, not getting; doing right, not wrong. And above all else, seek faith in God and faithfulness to God.

Put your heart where the real treasures are—God, people, giving, doing good. Then you'll always be a rich person, truly rich, not worldly rich!

Index of Scripture Texts